DOG N

RAW AND NATURAL FEEDING FOR A HEALTHY DOG

ANTHONY PORTOKALOGLOU

Copyright © 2017 by Anthony Portokaloglou

All rights reserved. No part of this publication may be reproduced, distributed or transmitted in any form or by any means, without prior written permission from the author.

Disclaimer Notice

The techniques described in this book are for informational purposes only. All attempts have been made by the author to provide real and accurate content. No responsibility will be taken by the author for any damages cost by misuse of the content described in this book. Please consult a licensed professional before utilizing the information of this book.

I hope you will enjoy this book. I would be very grateful if you would consider leaving a review!

Contents

INTRODUCTION 5

CHAPTER ONE: Call of the Wild- The History of Canine Nutrition 9

CHAPTER TWO: Domestication and the Modern Diet 14

CHAPTER THREE: What Did My Dog Just Eat? Commercial Food VS People Food VS Biscuits and Treats 19

CHAPTER FOUR: Obesity- most common canine health .. 41

CHAPTER FIVE: Dog food related allergies 46

CHAPTER SIX: Gastrointestinal (GI) Disorders- Explained 51

CHAPTER SEVEN: Dental Disease 55

CHAPTER EIGHT: From Puppies to Seniors – Specific Nutritional Needs 61

CHAPTER NINE: Balanced commercial food options 67

CHAPTER TEN: Raw food diets and Home cooking 70

CHAPTER ELEVEN: Special Needs Nutrition 77

CONCLUSION 85

INTRODUCTION

In the modern world, keeping our canine companions happy and healthy can be a jaunting and expensive commitment over the course of their lifetimes. According to a global survey of 22 countries conducted by GFK in 2016, 33% of people live with dogs. In the U.S., a 2017-2018 survey by the American Pet Products Association (APPA) revealed approximately 89.7 million dogs owned by 70% of households. With lifetime expectancies of 12-16 years for most canines, owners often underestimate the costs of providing for the health and nutritional needs of their furry family member.

Here in the U.S., we spend a lot of money on our dogs for both health and nutrition. As of 2017, the American Kennel Club (AKC) indicates routine canine veterinary costs range from $200-$500 per year depending on the size, age and health of your dog. This yearly cost does not include over the counter medications, dental cleanings and any emergencies or additional health issues that may arise.

Similarly, the US Pet Food Industry's most recent report shows that annual costs of dog food can range from $55-$235 depending on the size of your pet and type/quality of food being provided, although many owners argue that number can reach into the $500 range or more per year for bigger dogs. This estimated annual cost excludes biscuits, treats, supplements and medically prescribed foods, which can boost yearly costs to nearly $1000 for a single dog!

By examining the links between canine health and nutrition, pet owners will learn about the history of canine nutrition, the diseases related to poor or improper diets, and the various options that are available for the treatment, care and feeding of the nearly 90 million dogs here in the U.S. that provide joy, love and comfort in our daily lives.

CHAPTER ONE: Call of the Wild- The History of Canine Nutrition

Imagine walking the Earth nearly 15,000 years ago during the age of hunter-gatherers. At your side is your trusted companion – a slowly emerging domesticated canine, different from wolf-like ancestors in behavior but similar in its' prey drive and nutritional needs. What would your canine companion's diet look like? Experts such as veterinarians, archaeologists and canine food experts have been pondering that question for many years and it is only within the last few decades that advances in science have opened windows into the world of canine ancestral nutrition. The oldest known remains of what we refer to as a modern canine was discovered in Germany around 15,000 years ago. Buried with its humans, the Bonn-Oberkassel canine had all of the distinct bone features of a modern canine, and in 2013 DNA tests performed by the Hugo Obermaier Society positively confirmed the remains as Canis lupus familiaris i.e. dog. Unfortunately, most canine archaeological remains leave us little clue about the contents of their stomachs or their nutritional needs. For that, we need to look at the diets of their closest genetic relatives – wolves. According to Steve Brown, author of Unlocking the Canine Ancestral Diet, canines take after their wild wolf cousins as carnivores. The prey drive is their primary motivator, seeking out small animals and birds while hunting as individuals or capturing larger prey when hunting in packs. However, examinations of modern wolf excrement and remains also suggest that wolves are often omnivores and scavengers, seeking out what they need over time. Evidence of vegetables, fruits and grasses are often present next to protein bits digested from animal prey, but one type of food is noticeably absent: grains. L. David Mech, a noted wolf researcher, reports that wolves immediately consume just about every part of their animal prey starting with the larger organs first such as the heart, liver and kidneys before finishing with the bones. However, Mech noted that wolves will often ignore or discard any plant matter found in the intestines of their prey, supporting evidence that wolves and their wild canine counterparts do not ingest grains. A recent study published in the British Journal of Nutrition regarding the dietary nutrient profiles of wolves also found that they are "true carnivores consuming a negligible amount of vegetal matter". Over thousands of years there have been many factors other than ancestral traits which would account for the substance of a wild wolf's diet. Geography, environmental concerns, climate change, and natural prey extinction are certainly important things to consider when reviewing evidence of what wild wolves have naturally preferred to eat on a regular basis to keep them healthy and balanced. As a result, it is somewhat difficult to say with 100% certainty that the nutritional needs and cravings of domesticated canines in the last 15,000 years are a mirror image of their wild wolf counterparts, although there are enough similarities to provide a good starting point when discussing modern canine nutrition.

CHAPTER TWO: Domestication and the Modern Diet

Without a doubt, the biggest factor to be considered when looking at canine nutritional development is the role that human contact and companionship has played in a modern dog's diet. In fact, our development as hunter-gatherers allowed us to use food to domesticate the early canines. 15,000 years ago your canine companion would have also been your hunting partner, using its ancestral traits such as prey drive, scent, and agility to track and bring down food, which efforts you would have rewarded with a meal of scraps and bones. It is no wonder that over thousands of years the main association between dog and human has been focused on the human hand as a consistent source for nutrition. Following domestication, there is no doubt that early humans weren't particularly concerned with their dog's nutrition. Humans sought to satisfy their own needs by hunting or gathering things that were readily available to them. Being in part scavengers by nature, a dog's ancestral diet was certainly modified by the types of food made available to them by their human companions. According to The Lost History of the Canine Race by Mary Thurston, pre-industrial revolution dogs shared meals "identical to those of their peasant masters--meatless fare consisting of bread, potatoes, onions and boiled cabbage". Those masters who had greater wealth expanded the variety and nutritional value of the table food offered to their dogs. Thurston highlights historical examples of this trend, such as the provision of "shark's fins, curlews's livers and the breasts of quails..." to the Pekingese companion of the Chinese Empress or the feeding of "succulent bits of roast duck, consumme, cakes and candied nuts or fruit" to the dogs of the French Courts in the 1700's. Additionally, it is believed that canines, like their wild wolf cousins, could go 4 or 5 days between meals if conditions presented scarce opportunities for the capture of prey or the location of fruits and vegetables. Once the human-canine relationship was established, a human's need for food intake 1-2 times per day may have also modified a dog's natural eating schedule from large infrequent meals to smaller more frequent occurrences.

Over the centuries, humans became adept at using a canine's ancestral traits and prey drives to develop individual breeds centered around the types of food available in their geographic areas. Examples include retrievers for water fowl, pointers for field hunting, sight hounds for capture of small game, and terriers for underground detection and retrieval. The results of those activities often impacted what food a particular breed was given as part of its daily diet, and the effect was a further diversification of modern canine nutrition. Ultimately, as knowledge increased about the links between nutrition and human health, similar ideas were applied to dog health and nutrition. Now 15,000 years later, with your trusted canine companion still at your side, you must rely on your hunter-gatherer skills to make your way through the maze of theories and products to find the best approach for your dog's nutrition and health.

CHAPTER THREE: What Did My Dog Just Eat? Commercial Food VS People Food VS Biscuits and Treats

A. Commercial Food

Here in the U.S., it is clear from market statistics that the majority of us feed our dogs dry or wet foods prepared by national manufacturers. U.S. dry dog food sales from 2000-2014 totaled nearly $9.2 billion, with premium wet dog food sales in 2016 reaching $1.475 million. (source: Statista.com) The U.S is clearly the global leader in pet food sales, which means most studies and reports that have been prepared to date are often focused on the products and trends put out by U.S. manufacturers. Some base their ingredient contents on studies of pet health and nutrition, while others seem to focus on what inspires humans to buy a particular product, such as alluring packaging and advertising showing pictures of "happy dogs" which often skim over details of their product's nutritional value. So, what are the factors that drive us to purchase prepared foods for our dogs when we often spend so much time preparing our own human food? Why not do the same for our pets? Well as we've seen from pre-manufacturing history, humans spent a long time feeding their dogs similar foods to what they were eating. Some of those foods met the needs of their dog, but many foods did nothing nutritionally for either the human or their canine companion. As we advanced as a global industrial society in the 19th and 20th centuries our ideas about food and food preparation have changed greatly, not only for us but also for our dogs. Additionally, owners now often see their pets not solely as working or hunting companions, but as family members, trophy pets or even complimentary accessories to be pampered and doted on. According to a 2017 study on global pet care by Euromonitor International, modern pet food trends are often influenced by human diet goals such as vegetarianism, paleo diets, organic, low-carb, pro-biotic, non-GMO, etc..., or based on their views of pet ownership including convenience, cost, the desire to indulge with "goodies", and advertising that promotes products that are seen as similar to "premium" human foods with descriptions like "National"/ "Made in the USA", "Organic", "Limited Edition" or "Artisanal". The very first dog food manufacturer was in Great Britain. According to the Pet Food Institute, James Spratt developed the first mass produced dog biscuit in 1860, consisting of a mix of wheat meals, vegetables, beetroot and beef blood. His biscuits were such a large success that in 1890 production was begun in America, including the addition of some types of dry kibble. By 1922, the first canned food, Ken-L Ration, was added to the trend of manufactured products. It consisted of horsemeat and followed the common practice where historically, according to The Whole Dog Journal, "canned dog foods were a handy place to utilize parts of food-animal carcasses that couldn't be used in human food products, ingredients with the anonymous designation of "meat" or the even more dubious "meat byproducts." In particular, horsemeat was a staple of canned dog food for many years to follow until changes in most U.S. laws banned the use of it in animal products. We've come a long way since the early 20th century when it comes to the proliferation of dog food manufacturers. As of 2017, the top two leading dry dog food manufacturers in the U.S. commanded a whopping 67.7% of the market share, producing more than 50 individual brands of dry dog to the commercial and veterinary sectors (source: Statista.com). One contributing factor to the popularity of these top two manufacturers, apart from nutritional considerations, may be that their mass-produced pet foods fit into an owner's "convenience" factor, as most of these labels are available in general grocery markets where human food is also purchased. The same trend regarding convenience also applies when looking at the top producers of canned (wet) dog foods in the U.S. The ingredients and nutritional values of the top brands of dog food vary greatly, leaving pet owners with conflicting information when deciding which product(s) to feed to their dogs. Let's look at the ingredient label from one of the top selling dry food brands: "Ground yellow corn, chicken by-product meal, corn gluten meal, whole wheat flour, animal fat preserved with mixed-tocopherols (form of Vitamin E), rice flour, beef, soy flour, sugar, propylene glycol, meat and bone meal, tricalcium phosphate, phosphoric acid, salt, water, animal digest, sorbic acid (a preservative), potassium chloride, dried carrots, dried peas, calcium propionate (a preservative), L-Lysine monohydrochloride, choline chloride, added color (Red 40, Yellow 5, Yellow 6, Blue 2), DL-Methionine, Vitamin E supplement, zinc sulfate, ferrous sulfate, manganese sulfate, niacin, Vitamin A supplement, calcium carbonate, copper sulfate, Vitamin B-12 supplement, calcium pantothenate, thiamine mononitrate, garlic oil, pyridoxine hydrochloride, riboflavin supplement, Vitamin D-3 supplement, *menadione sodium bisulfite complex (source of Vitamin K activity), calcium iodate, folic acid, biotin, sodium selenite."

And here's a look at the label from one of the leading wet food brands:

Sufficient Water for processing, Beef By-products, Animal Liver, Meat By-products, Chicken, Chicken By-products, Calcium Carbonate, Sodium Tripolyphospate, Carrageen, Added Color, Potassium Chloride, Xanthan Gum, Magnesium Proteinate, Dried Yam, Natural Flavor, Salt, Erythorbic Acid, Grilled Chicken Flavor, Guar gum, Zinc Sulfate, Vitamin E Supplement, Monocalcium phosphate, Copper Sulfate, Sodium Nitrate (for color retention), d-Calcium Pantothenate, Thiamine Mononitrate (Vitamin B1), Vitamin A Supplement, Vitamin D3 Supplement.

Do you recognize many of these ingredients? Most consumers don't, leaving the nutrition of their dogs in the hands of manufacturers who have latitude in the amount and type of ingredients they can include in their products. Let's look at a few of the ingredients listed above that are considered harmful or less than desirable for your pet's nutrition, keeping in mind that the ingredients are listed in descending order by volume/quantity.

The ingredient labels above reference "chicken by-product meal", "beef by-products", "animal liver" and "meat by-products" with little explanation as to the sources of the actual contents that make up each group. For decades dog foods have generally included more animal by-products than meat as the main protein ingredients. Those animal by-products, according to the Association of American Feed Control Officials (AAFCO), "include parts obtained from any animals which have died from sickness or disease". The types of animals that are often included range from goats, pigs, and horses, to rats and animals euthanized at shelters. It can also include bodily fluids, diseased organs, and decomposed tissues. Ann Martin, the author of Foods Dogs Die For, argues that manufacturers often hide the sources of animal meal and by-products: "Dead-stock removal operations play a major role in the pet food industry. Dead animals, road kill that cannot be buried at roadside, and in some cases, zoo animals, are picked up by these dead stock operations" and find their way into commercial pet food production. Most of the time, meat that humans would find fit for consumption is included in a very low quantity or not at all. Another prevalent ingredient, especially in the dry dog food example, is the addition of various grains as sources of fiber and carbohydrates. Items such as "Ground yellow corn", "whole wheat flour", "rice flour", and "soy flour" are ingredients that many experts believe are the leading causes of allergies and stomach disorders. According to caninejournal.com, "dogs have little natural digestive support for breaking down and metabolizing complex carbohydrates and cereal grains. These difficult-to-digest fibers and grains remain undigested, with the body relying mainly on fermentation to break them down." Additionally, some critics point to the use of animal grade feed as the source of grain in dog foods, not the higher end USDA inspected human grade grains we put on our tables. Grain fillers can also be used to increase the amount of bulk or fiber in the food, but these fillers also have little to zero nutritional benefit. There are also a whole host of chemicals that are included in many commercial dog foods, such as "propylene glycol" (antifreeze), preservatives made from pesticides used on fruit and grains such as "ethoxyquin", or synthetic substances such as "menadione sodium bisulfite complex" which deliver vitamins but have been shown to also have potential carcinogenic effects according to the Material Safety Data Sheets that accompany their production. And let's not forget listed ingredients such as sugars, food colorings, and animal "digest" used as flavoring agents. While humans may care about the color of their food, it is unlikely that your dog does - what matters most to them is smell and flavor. The use of flavoring agents may be a smart move on the part of manufacturers to get your dog to like their product, but it doesn't necessarily mean that the product contains quality ingredients that would produce the natural flavors our pups desire. While some studies indicate that dog food labeled as "premium" is now the primary driving force in sales in the U.S., what is and what is not premium is often just a matter of packaging as opposed to a variance in the actual ingredients used in production. Even products that were initially created by smaller manufacturers as "artisanal" have now been bought out by large producers, creating more confusion over whether the ingredients used really vary between labels once they are produced under the same roof. Commercial dog food production has changed, especially in the last two decades or so -- but even with the advent of premium packaging it may be that the answer to the question "What did my dog just eat?" will contain the same ingredients that have been part of the last 80 years of commercial canine food production. For many dog owners, factors such as cost and convenience keep them from investigating other food manufacturers and products that could provide a true premium nutritional benefit for their beloved pooch. And for other owners, manufactured food just isn't the ticket for their canine companions.

B. People Food

Health, nutrition, socialization and satisfaction – these factors are most often behind a human's pursuit of a particular food. Eating an ice cream on a hot day, slurping up soup when we're sick, or munching on a pizza with friends – all these scenarios highlight the complicated relationship we have with our food. However, most of these factors mean little to our canine friends – at least on the surface. Their relationship with food is driven by hunger and satisfied by any food that their senses perceive as being appropriate to the task. They certainly are not social eaters who like eating with their "friends", since competition for food is a basic survival instinct. And while their bodily functions may provide us with some clue as to their health and nutrition, they are not able to communicate verbally with us as to which foods make them feel good or which ones they prefer to eat. Instead, humans often make those decisions for their pets, especially when it comes to what people food we find satisfying that we then share with them from our table or include in their diets. Before the recent advent of nutritionally based homemade pet foods and raw diets, most modern pet owners (like their historical counterparts) saw little harm in sharing their bounties with their canine family members. Common refrains heard in households all over the country – "let him lick the bowl", "give her some of the crust" or "it's just a little left over" –

become symphonies played out in the mouths of our dogs. Patterns of food-seeking and begging emerge in association with the smells of human food and our regular habits of giving it to them, creating not only nutritional but behavior problems as well. Human food producers often put in chemicals, preservatives and spices to help us with the satisfaction element of our desire for a particular food. High sodium levels, spicy seasonings, heavy carbohydrate counts and fat levels --- all these traits in our food are passed on to our dogs. And just like humans, these food traits often satisfy the senses that dogs use to determine what tastes good to them. Since canine behavior is often driven by their senses, it is no wonder that many dogs exposed to human food on a regular basis convince their owners that the only food they will eat is that which also tastes good to us.

C. Biscuits and Treats

No examination of what our dogs eat would be complete without a look at the types of biscuits and treats that have been the mainstay of pet food manufacturers for many years. Treats can be supplements for nutrition, as well as provide behavioral stimuli during training. But for the most part, biscuits and treats have been used by humans as a sign of love and affection toward their dogs with little thought being put into whether the manufactured products are healthy and beneficial. As we looked at previously, the earliest mass-produced dog food by James Spratt was in the form of a biscuit.

Manufacturers soon learned that they could diverge their product lines by turning biscuits and treats into a separate food category, generating new revenues and satisfying the human desire to reward their dogs with snacks in much the same way that humans reward themselves. What started out as biscuit has now transitioned into cookies, soft chews, rawhides and the treats that resemble people food like bacon and pepperoni. According to a study conducted in 2017, "sales of pet treats have outpaced both dog and cat food over the last five years, with treats sales increasing by 29 percent between 2012-17 to reach $4.39 billion" (Mintel.com). Just like manufactured dog foods, the nutritional value of dog biscuits and treats can vary greatly depending on the quality of ingredients used in production. Many contain by-products, grains, colorings, preservatives and additives designed to enhance the look, smell and taste so that our pets will respond favorably when presented with them. In the wake of several treat recalls in the past decade due to harmful substances, pet owners are more in tune with looking for labels that say "Made in USA" as a way of ensuring that the ingredients are sourced under stricter laws than some ingredients obtained overseas. However, as we've seen with domestically produced dog foods, there is a lot of variance in the quality of ingredients used so that solely relying on where the treats are produced may not be the only safeguard in providing your dogs with healthy treats and snacks. There are many types of treats available— some manufactured and some natural — and they come in all forms, including crunchy, soft, freeze-dried, jerky, rawhides, animal bones, pizzles, and pig's ears. What type of treat your dog wants to eat or can eat often depends on age, health, activity level and general flavor inclinations — much like their human owners. And we should not forget those surprise treats that seem to be the favorite of every dog — the bit of human food that lands on the ground such as the stray potato chip, a couple of peanuts, or that remaining bite of cheese. Our households are smorgasbords for the attentive and discerning pup intent on supplementing their regular diets with enticing human treats that make their way into the canine world at our feet. It is at that point that we often shift our focus from the question of "What did my dog just eat" to the question of "What effect will that have on my pet's health?".

CHAPTER FOUR: Obesity- most common canine health

How Does My Dog Feel?

The link between canine health and nutrition is a complicated one, although experts agree on one thing: the most common canine health problems can be directly traced to what we are feeding our furry companions. We've all had those days with our dogs, cleaning up the carpet after a moment of vomiting or stomach upset. Those are often the easy signs of the link between food and health. But what about less obvious symptoms such as sneezing, ear scratching, bad breath, skin itching, hair loss, or listlessness? Are these the product of disease and/or genetics? Or could these symptoms be the result of inappropriate nutrition? Let's take a look at the most common canine health issues and what experts tell us about their connection to the things our dogs are ingesting on a daily basis.

A. Obesity

Canine obesity, like human obesity, is simply referred to as "a nutritional disease which is defined by an excess of body fat" and "common in dogs of all ages, but it usually occurs in middle-aged dogs, and generally in those that are between the ages of 5 and 10." (petmd.com). A 2017 survey conducted of 1,215 pet owners and 544 veterinary professionals by the Association for Pet Obesity Prevention (APOP) found that a whopping 56% of dogs in the U.S. are clinically obese! Why are we concerned about obesity in our pets? Well for virtually the same reason that we are concerned about it in ourselves – health. Heart disease, diabetes, respiratory impairments, torn ligaments, arthritis and generally reduced life spans are the result of "excessive food intake and insufficient exercise", according to experts at the American Animal Hospital Association (AAHA). We know that, unlike humans, dogs are not stress eaters and don't have the ability to whip up something on the stove or order a pizza. Therefore, their issues with eating and weight fall squarely on the shoulders of us, their owners, who are the providers of food and exercise on a daily basis. Nutritionally, dogs that are fed snacks, table scraps and homemade foods are the most likely to become obese vs. dogs that are fed better quality commercial dry or wet foods (AAHA). And without a doubt, our busy lives and crowded cities often make it difficult for us to provide enough exercise to counteract the negative health effects caused by excessive or nutritionally inadequate food intake. The survey by APOP in 2017 highlighted the confusion that some owners and even veterinarians feel about the effect of different types of food (raw, dry, organic, etc...) on dog weight, although both agreed overwhelmingly (65%) that people food was "unhealthy" for their pets. This confusion in part is generated by the variety of sources that owners and professionals use to obtain information on the nutritional value of the foods readily available in pet stores and grocery markets – sources such as other veterinary professionals, sales representatives of pet food producers, the internet, trainers, breeders and family/friends. But while the sheer volume of information out there may present challenges to deciphering attractive marketing terms like "premium", "organic" or "healthy", the only definitive way to measure the nutritional value of the foods we feed our dogs is to monitor their weight and physical functioning on a regular basis and adjust their food intake and exercise accordingly.

CHAPTER FIVE: Dog food related allergies

From time to time, we've all witnessed our dogs scratching/shaking their ears, chewing on a "hot spot" on their skin, or having diarrhea after eating. Our first reaction, often spurred on by the claims of specialty dog food brands, is to immediately target a food allergy as the source of the infection or discomfort. In response we change the dog food that we are using, which works for a while until our pups' symptoms return -- then we repeat the pattern by changing the food again. Why doesn't this strategy ultimately work for our dogs? A look at the medicine behind food allergies highlights the complicated strategy for defining and detecting those allergies in our pets. According to the Cummings Veterinary Medical Center at Tufts University, "Food allergies occur when an animal's immune system misidentifies a protein from a food as an invader rather than a food item and mounts an immune response". What this means is that a dogs' body goes on the defense when attacked by a food ingredient – and often loses that defense in the form of ear and skin infections or gastrointestinal upset. The most common food allergies for dogs are contained in animal proteins such as chicken, soy, eggs, or beef and therefore, according to many experts, grains such as wheat or corn are not causes of food allergies since they don't contain those specific proteins. Dogs can become allergic over time, at any time, and in response to any form of animal protein found in most commercially manufactured pet foods. Even attempts at feeding our dogs more exotic proteins are no guarantee: "Feeding a diet with duck, kangaroo, lamb, or venison doesn't prevent food allergies, it just makes it likely that if your pet develops one, it will be to that protein instead of something more common like pork or chicken." (vetnutrition.Tufts.edu). So, what is the best way to determine if your pet's allergy symptoms are caused by food? Unfortunately, there are no blood tests that can make that determination, but there is one way relied on by most veterinarians to diagnose a true food allergy: an elimination and challenge diet trial. In a nutshell, this consists of removing all regular food ingredients from your pets' diet and replacing it with a food source they have never been exposed to – the theory being that a dog will not react to something completely new since it takes time to develop a food allergy. After a short period on the new diet when symptoms and infections have been eliminated, your dog is returned to their original food to see if the symptoms re-occur. If so, it is likely that your dog has an allergy to one or more of the ingredients in that food. Repeat trials are performed to narrow down the offending ingredients and eliminate them completely from your pets' daily cuisine. (veterinarymedicine.dvm360.com). In reality, food related allergies in dogs are less common than most people think -- only about 10% of all dog allergy cases can be related to food while most other allergy symptoms are caused by the dreaded flea or environmental factors. When food is the culprit, changing to a different commercial food may provide some form of interim relief but ultimately it will not be a permanent solution, since most of the available replacement products contain some type of animal protein that could be the source of the next allergy to develop. It is important for owners of dogs with food allergies to examine the ingredients of commercially manufactured dog foods and treats, especially those brands that claim that their foods consist of allergy-free ingredients.

CHAPTER SIX: Gastrointestinal (GI) Disorders- Explained

Any dog owner knows that one of the most common reasons for a visit to the vet's office is to deal with the oft-turbulent tummy upset. Vomiting, gas, diarrhea – just a few of the symptoms that cause our dogs pain and discomfort. When it comes to canine nutrition, proper "digestion is critical not only for providing nutrients but also for maintaining the proper balance of fluid and electrolytes (salts) in the body" (merckvetmanual.com).

It's fairly easy to diagnose when a dog's symptoms are caused by the ingestion of something that is not food. Bones, socks, balls, rocks, pantyhose, underwear, toys, corn cobs, sticks and hair ties are the top 10 items most often extracted from the insides of our pups (iheartdogs.com). Additional causes of gastrointestinal issues in dogs can include bacterial infections, parasites and viruses – most of which can be detected through blood work, lab tests and diagnostic imaging. These various causes can usually be addressed and treated through medications that can help to restore full digestive functioning. (merckvetmanual.com) But what about GI symptoms that cannot be explained by one of the above causes? The best remaining explanation points to a food 'intolerance', which is to be distinguished from a food 'allergy' since it does not involve an immune system reaction, although the symptoms are often identical. Food intolerances involve reactions to particular ingredients, contaminants, food colorings, and additives such as propylene glycol (petmd.com). And unlike food allergies, food intolerances can include reactions to grains such as wheat and corn, which are notoriously hard for dogs to digest for nutrient absorption. This is where foods labeled as "grain-free" can be a beneficial alternative for dogs with grain intolerances. Food intolerances are detected in the same manner as food allergies – by use of a diet elimination and challenge trial – and then treated in the same manner by changing foods and eliminating any ingredients that are suspects in the discomfort of our dogs. Unfortunately, many dogs experience relapses of their symptoms due to the lack of strict adherence to the new diet by their owners, who don't always stop to consider the ramifications that just one or two non-approved treats can cause. Ultimately, GI disorders in dogs can be medically treated and managed effectively through a proper diet tailored to avoid the symptoms of food intolerance, while still reserving some room for us to spoil our pups appropriately.

CHAPTER SEVEN: Dental Disease

Perhaps the biggest culprit effecting canine health and nutrition is dental disease – however, it is also an issue that is the easiest for owners to address and correct. The problem is so common that the American Veterinary Dental College (AVDC.org) estimates that most dogs will experience some form of periodontal disease by the time they are three, although symptoms don't often surface until much later and sometimes too late to prevent more serious health conditions from developing as a result. According to the AVDC, "Periodontal disease begins when bacteria in the mouth form a substance called plaque that sticks to the surface of the teeth. Subsequently, minerals in the saliva harden the plaque into dental calculus (tartar), which is firmly attached to the teeth……The real problem develops as plaque and calculus spread under the gum line. Bacteria in this 'sub-gingival' plaque set in motion a cycle of damage……." This tartar, left untreated or undertreated, can lead to serious health problems, such as heart, kidney and liver diseases, diabetes, GI disorders and lung disorders. According to holistic veterinarian Karen Becker: "These serious health concerns develop or are made worse by the constant presence of oral bacteria flushing into the bloodstream through inflamed or bleeding gum tissue" (dogsnaturallymagazine.com). Some dog breeds, especially smaller ones, are pre-disposed to dental disease by sheer virtue of the crowded nature of their small mouths and teeth.

However, all dogs experience some degree of oral disease requiring regular maintenance at home and at the vet's office. Once periodontal disease has spread past the point where home therapies will work, more extensive measures may be required, such as professional dental cleaning under anesthesia, extractions of rotted teeth, and treatment with antibiotics to clear up any bacterial infections. The AVDC has issued a firm statement that they advise against cleaning treatments that do not occur under anesthesia as they do not perform the deep dental scaling necessary to eliminate tartar and bacteria below the gum lines. (AVDC.org) How does nutrition effect the development of dental disease in our dogs? Many veterinarians disagree on whether particular types of food play a part or whether regular hygiene is the more determining factor. As we've examined, regular hygiene maintenance at home and at the vet's office is a crucial element ensuring the long-term health of our pets. But what about food? A study by a Tom Lonsdale, D.V.M. looked at whether dry kibble foods caused more dental disease than raw diets. In his opinion, dogs that ate strictly dry food had more visible tartar/ plaque build-up in their mouths and bleeding gums than dogs who were fed a raw diet which included raw marrow bones to chew on. Why? As veterinarian Sarah Chapman concludes, dry kibble foods contain starches and sugars that easily attach themselves to dental surfaces and below tissues, and dogs rarely chew their kibble enough to get some "scrubbing" action on their teeth as they eat. Raw diets, on the other hand, often don't contain ingredients that will stick to dental surfaces, and the addition of raw meaty bones provides the necessary friction to clean the tartar away. (dogsnaturallymagazine.com) What is clear from the presence of dental disease in our dogs is that it is a common problem that can only be addressed by regular veterinarian examinations and home maintenance, including the addition of raw meaty bones or dental chews to act as a tasty substitute for the more mundane toothbrush. Protecting the health of our pups' mouths is the first step in protecting their overall health. As we've seen in the cases of obesity, allergies, GI disorders and dental disease, the links between canine health and nutrition are strong and definitive. The old saying that is applied to computers, "garbage in – garbage out", could easily be applied to what we are feeding our pets on a regular basis. Our best course of action as owners is to engage all segments of our pups' health by feeding them in appropriate amounts, exercising them regularly, performing regular physical inspections of their teeth and bodies, and providing them with the right type of food that will allow them the maximum amount of nutrient absorption throughout their lives.

CHAPTER EIGHT: From Puppies to Seniors – Specific Nutritional Needs

What Should My Dog Eat

The information regarding dog food and diets can be overwhelming, confusing and contradictory -- to say the least. It has been suggested by numerous studies that very few dog owners understand the nutritional needs of their canine best friends, and the immense tide of information certainly does not help that cause. However, breaking down the nutritional requirements that our dogs need to be healthy and happy at various stages in their lives gets us closer to finding, or making, the perfect foods for our furry companions. According to a 2006 report on the Nutrient Requirements of Dogs and

Cats issued by the National Research Council as part of its studies on animal nutrition, it is scientifically accepted that dogs require nutrients on a daily basis from the following categories: proteins, fats, minerals, vitamins, and carbohydrates – and of course water. While the amount of the nutrients from each category often depends on the stage of life and specific health concerns, the essentials remain the same for optimum health. Each category of nutrients in a dog's diet have specific functions that unite to serve their overall health. One of the most important nutrients is protein, which provides more than half of the essential amino acids dogs need for healthy tissues and muscles. Approximately 10% of a dog's daily intake should consist of proteins such as meat and fish, and puppies often need nearly twice the amount of protein required by an adult or senior dog. Failure to provide the proper amount of protein can result in 'deficiencies' that cause hair loss, skin problems and other health issues (petmd.com). The same can be said for the addition of fats and fatty acids in the diets of our dogs. Fats are derived primarily from plant oils and meat sources, providing energy, skin/hair conditioning and improving the flavor of the commercially prepared foods that they eat. As with proteins, a diet consisting of approximately 5-10% in fat and fatty acids is appropriate for most dogs without causing additional issues with obesity, and puppies also need a higher amount of fat intake during the earlier stages of development. (http://dels.nas.edu/banr).

Minerals and vitamins are important for the development and functioning of all living beings, especially dogs. While humans can supplement missing minerals and vitamins with the direct intake of pills and over the counter products, dogs must obtain all their vitamins and minerals directly from their food sources. The report on animal nutrition by the National Research Council, Nutrient Requirements of Dogs and Cats, lists 12 minerals such as potassium, magnesium and calcium to promote strong teeth and bones, cell and muscle development, and proper functioning of the organs and glands. Similarly, dogs require small doses of several vitamins such as A, D and E to protect the development and functioning of their vision, heart, and immune systems. Both vitamins and minerals can be found naturally in the meat and vegetable ingredients of dog foods, as well as in supplements added by food manufacturers. Lastly, carbohydrates, including starches and sugars, make up the bulk of the nutrient content for most dog diets – approximately 50%. Carbohydrates, combined with proteins and fats, provide the daily energy our dogs need and contribute to healthy weight maintenance. According to the animal nutrition study by the National Research Council, digestible carbohydrates are broken down into "fermentable" and "non-fermentable" fibers, with fermentable fibers such as "certain starches and dietary fibers" assisting with the "regulation of blood glucose concentrations and enhance immune function" while non-fermentable fibers "such as cellulose and wheat bran, contribute little in terms of energy or nutrition" (http://dels.nas.edu/banr). The overfeeding or underfeeding of carbohydrates can lead to many health problems, and while puppies start out needing nearly twice as much caloric intake as their adult counterparts for proper development, senior dogs need about 20% less in order to avoid obesity and joint-related issues. The main lessons when looking at the nutritional needs of dogs are (1) to recognize the various health and development impacts that improper nutrition can have on the health of our dogs, and (2) to stay vigilant as our dogs age to make sure that we adjust their nutrient intakes to meet the needs of their particular stage of life.

CHAPTER NINE: Balanced commercial food options

Now that we have an understanding of the scientific-based nutritional needs of our canine companions, the next step is to look at the various commercial food products that many of us use for our dogs on a daily basis. While there are many factors such as cost and convenience that influence which brands we buy, the current market statistics clearly show a trend toward the purchase of foods labeled "balanced", "natural" or "grain-free". In the U.S., 69% of all dog food sales had a focus on the "natural market" (GFK, 2015), although what "natural" really means on package labeling is not exactly clear. Under the set of nutritional guidelines set forth by AAFCO, the term "natural" refers to the types of preservatives used in dog foods; it does not refer to the types of ingredients used in processing. However, the general belief by most dog owners is that "natural" is the same as "grain-free", a belief spurred on by the packaging of many pet foods. Since much has come to light in recent years regarding digestion issues with dog foods heavy in non-fermentable fibers such as wheat bran, the sales of foods labeled as "grain-free" will continue to dominate the market (GFK, 2017), despite the scientific evidence that dogs need some types starches and carbohydrates for energy production and glucose regulation. So exactly what does a "balanced" dog food consist of? Dog foods labeled "complete and balanced" meet all the minimum and maximum standards established by AAFCO, which takes into account the scientific research of the various nutrient categories required for optimal canine health. But as stated in chapter two, the interpretation of those standards by food manufacturers as to their sources of proteins (including road kill), carbohydrates (corn, wheat), and other additives leaves questions regarding whether their products are truly healthy and balanced for our pets. In the end, owners should reject commercial dog foods that contain many of the artificial preservatives, flavors, fillers or by-products discussed in chapter two and focus on foods that meet all the nutrient categories with high quality proteins, highly digestible carbohydrates, and naturally sourced vitamins/minerals.

CHAPTER TEN: Raw food diets and Home cooking

The history of canine nutrition starts with raw food – from their pre-domestication days as wild animals through the development of the first commercially manufactured foods. The trend away from raw foods and towards manufactured dog foods became predominant as humans became more dependent on commercially prepared foods as part of their daily intake. However, in 1993 an Australian veterinarian by the name of Ian Billinghurst made a revolutionary suggestion: feed dogs a raw diet consisting of the same items that they ate prior to domestication. He called this diet "BARF", which stands for "Bones and Raw Food" or "Biologically Appropriate Raw Food", and consists of "raw animal protein (meat, bones and offal), raw vegetables and fruit, raw whole eggs, yoghurt, kelp and healthy fresh herbs" (barfaustralia.com) It was his theory that by feeding dogs what their bodies were biologically meant to digest, health issues such as gastrointestinal disorders, skin problems, dental disease and obesity could be eliminated. Ideally, a proper raw food diet will contain all the recommended categories and percentages of the basic nutrients that dogs need for healthy lives. For a BARF diet, proper pre-domestication percentages include 70% muscle meat, 10% raw meaty bones, 10% organs (liver being half) and 10% fruits, veggies and/or dairy (since the belief is that canines are omnivores, not strict carnivores). Other raw food preparations use "prey model" percentages which include "80 – 85% muscle meat, 10 – 15% raw meaty bones and 5- 10% organs & offal (with half of this amount being liver), excluding all plant matter, fruit and grains with the belief that canines are strict carnivores. Prey model diets also focus on feeding pieces of whole prey as opposed to ground meat from domesticated livestock (primalpooch.com). There is also a split of opinion when it comes to the term "balanced"- whether that means every meal should be balanced or whether there is "balance over time" with providing a variety of foods during the course of the week. (therawfeedingcommunity.com). Considering the amount of unnecessary additives and potentially harmful source ingredients contained in commercially manufactured foods, Billinghurst's ideas for raw food diets spread, causing an explosion of new products on the natural pet foods market. However, in 2015 a series of recalls of raw food brands occurred due to issues with bacteria contamination, such as e-coli and salmonellas. These recalls caused consumers to re-evaluate whether raw food diets are safe and appropriate for their pets and caused similar disagreements within the veterinarian communities. Today, new guidelines for contamination and safety issues have revived the raw food market and there are many brands and varieties of commercially produced raw foods in all forms, including freeze dried and dehydrated products. Most are based on the BARF model since it is the easiest to source and reduce to commercial packaging. Those pet owners who make the decision to make their own homemade dog foods, raw or otherwise, can find a plethora of recipes on the internet for making balanced nutritional options for their furry friends. Experts stress that understanding the basic nutrient needs of canines and supplementing their diets with appropriate vitamins and minerals will help owners avoid the pitfalls and problems that appear as a result of nutritional deficiencies. A 2014 study conducted by the veterinary hospital at Sao Paulo University on the nutritional results of homemade diets showed that only 46 of the original 59 owners in the study kept their pets on the prescribed homemade diet, and out of those 46 owners: "30.4% admitted they had changed the recipe, 40% did not adequately control the amount of provided ingredients, 73.9% did not use the recommended amounts of soybean oil and salt and 28.3% did not use the vitamin, mineral, or amino acid supplements" (petmd.com). Clearly those owners who feed raw diets, regardless of the model chosen, will need to make a commitment to ensuring that their preparations are meeting their dog's nutritional needs and adding to their pup's health with additional benefits such as clean teeth from raw bones and control of obesity with less carbohydrates. Owners should note that gastrointestinal issues can arise if the transition to a raw food diet is not done slowly. Experts suggest starting with more bland proteins like fish or chicken and mixing in some of your dog's previous commercially produced food until they are totally weaned onto the new diet with no GI issues (therawfeedingcommunity.com).

CHAPTER ELEVEN: Special Needs Nutrition

Unlike canine owners of the pre-20th century past, modern medical technologies have allowed veterinary and pet nutrition specialists to study issues of dog health and their links to proper nutrition. While some owners and experts claim that certain diets or foods can prevent diseases like cancers or disorders like hip dysplasia, most of the special needs dog foods focus on addressing issues like allergies, obesity and senior pet care. Some commercially produced special needs diets are handled exclusively by veterinarians, who have the expertise to match a dog's health issues to a specific mix of ingredients designed to address or lessen the symptoms being experienced. These range from serious health matters like kidney or liver disease to less complicated matters such as allergies and obesity. These prescribed foods have undergone extensive testing to ensure that their ingredients have some scientific basis for addressing the issues they are prescribed for. In the U.S. this certification is done by the Center for Veterinary Medicine (whole-dog-journal.com). Over-the-counter foods labeled as specially designed for one issue or another are not required to undergo the testing certification of medically prescribed foods. They are usually designed to address one of four issues: allergies, obesity, puppy nutrition, and senior dog care. The latter two categories, as previously discussed, deal primarily with the changing nutritional needs of dogs during different stages of life development. Puppy foods have higher carbohydrate/caloric levels and protein percentages to meet the exuberant energy needs and developing bone structures of our young canine companions. Conversely, senior foods scale back the fat and calories to avoid issues with obesity, heart diseases and diabetes, and often include more digestible carbohydrates to deal with the aging GI systems of our most beloved senior furry family members. Based on what we know about dog nutrition, most of these over-the-counter foods for puppies and seniors are adequate in addressing their specific generational needs. The conflicts that often arise regarding special needs diets occur when discussing over-the-counter foods that claim they address allergies and obesity. Most "hypoallergenic" dog foods claim that status based on the absence of grains from their products. However, we know that problems with grain in dog foods are a tolerance issue while most true dog food allergies are protein allergies, which means that grain free foods can still be allergic triggers for dogs. So, while products that are labeled merely as "grain free" foods can help with GI problems associated with intolerance, food products that are labeled as "L.I.D. – Limited Ingredient Diet" can be more successful in controlling both the myriad of skin and itching problems caused by protein allergies and GI issues associated with grain intolerances. Most L.I.D. foods will avoid the following major allergy triggers: beef, dairy, chicken, lamb, fish, corn, wheat, soy, and yeast; additionally, many will eliminate grains that are the sources of food intolerances. Even with these limited ingredients, many experts recommend changing your dog's food periodically to address any developing allergies that may occur after a lengthy exposure to a particular type of protein. As for those doggy tummies that stick out a little too far, lo-calorie foods abound in the over-the-counter market. According to How to Help Your Overweight Dog Lose Weight written by veterinarian Donna Spector, "Obesity is frequently indicative that our dogs are sedentary, couch potato eating machines burning almost no calories". Her theory on dog weight loss is simple: "Your dog must eat less — and exercise more" (petmd.com). Without a doubt that holds true – both for humans and our canine companions. Our reliance on pre-packaged human foods full of heavy doses of fats and carbohydrates translates down the chain to the pre-packaged foods we feed our dogs, and with little exercise, those foods quickly add to the ever-growing problem of obesity across all segments of our society. Lo-cal dog food options can help owners address one-half of the problem by reducing the amount of calories and fats that our pets are consuming on a daily basis. In a commercially produced lo-cal dog food, this is often done by including a large amount of carbohydrate fillers that attempt to make your pup feel full quicker, thus reducing the amount they need to eat. Unfortunately, this results in meals that are unbalanced nutritionally and impact healthy stool production/frequency.

Further, the full feeling tends to dissipate quickly, leaving owners in the position of giving their dogs treats in response to frequent begging requests. Since many over-the-counter treats are loaded with sugars, chemicals, and fats, the lo-cal diet becomes ineffective and the dog remains obese. In her article regarding canine weight loss, Dr. Spector suggests a successful diet food (and treats) that contains three things: "above-average protein, below-average fat, and below-average calories" (petmd.com). That applies to commercially produced foods as well as homemade diets although generally speaking, dogs that are fed raw food diets tend to have less issues with obesity than dogs fed manufactured foods. In addition to low-calorie foods that meet Dr. Spector's recommendations, owners can include natural treats that are low-fat and tasty, such as carrots, steamed green beans, or apple slices (minus the seeds). Combined with regular exercise, this type of local diet should result in a weight loss of 3%-5% of your dog's total weight per month and add years of companionship for you and your furry friend to enjoy.

CONCLUSION

Fifteen thousand years ago our human ancestors probably did not have significant thoughts or discussions regarding the health and nutritional needs of their canine sidekicks, who exchanged their hunting skills for a leftover scrap of bone or meat from their human partners. Fast forward in time to the present, where the human-canine connection has been changed over the centuries due to domestication of the dog as our companions and work partners, as well as due to the technological advances that created the ability to mass produce pet food for our convenience. Scientific advances have also increased our knowledge of the nutritional and health needs of dogs, providing us with the tools to help our dogs lead healthy and happy lives. In economic terms, the resulting markets that have arisen to provide those tools and resources demonstrate that owners have clearly been willing to invest millions of dollars to meet the needs of their furry friends. The bond between humans and our canine companions is undeniable – we provide them with affection, care and attention and in return they provide us with love, support, and even entertainment. It is a bond that owners must nurture by ensuring that their pets eat foods that meet nutritional needs, provide regular exercise to maintain health, and provide regular veterinary care to monitor their progress as they grow and develop from puppies to senior dogs. In the end, it is a massive commitment and responsibility for owners, but as any dog owner will tell you, it is one that is repaid tenfold with just one wag of your best friend's tail.

Made in the USA
Las Vegas, NV
23 February 2021